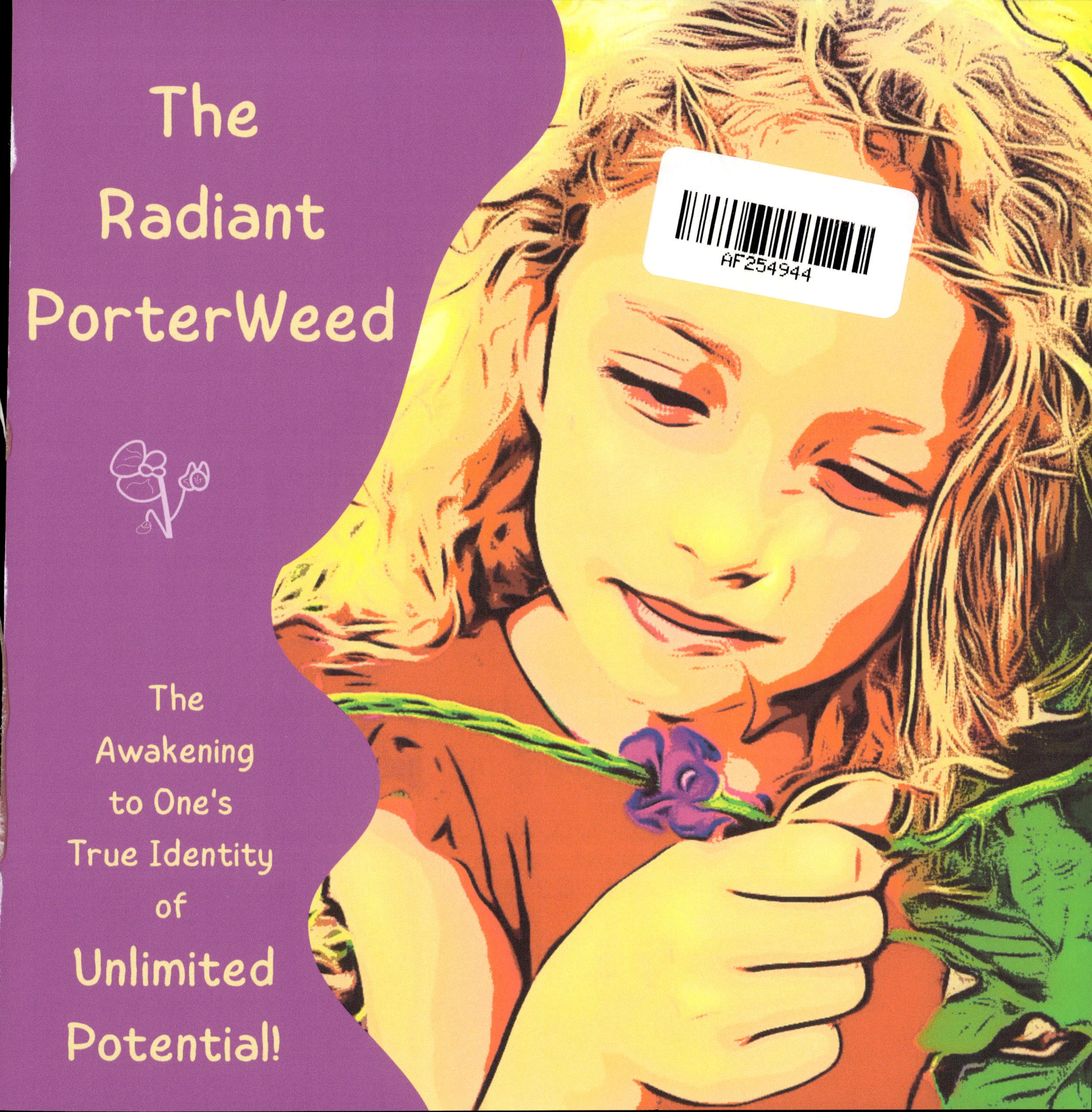

The Radiant PorterWeed
The Awakening to One's True Identity of Unlimited Potential!
AF254944

THE RADIANT PORTERWEED: THE AWAKENING TO ONE'S TRUE IDENITY OF UNLIMITED POTENTIAL

Dedication

To the family I was born into and the family of Soul*Dancers I joined along the way- MyRadiant Cluster- THANK YOU SO MUCH FOR PLAYING HUMAN WITH ME- WITH ALL MY LOVE, LIGHT, & JOY

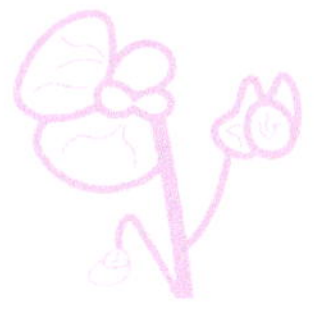

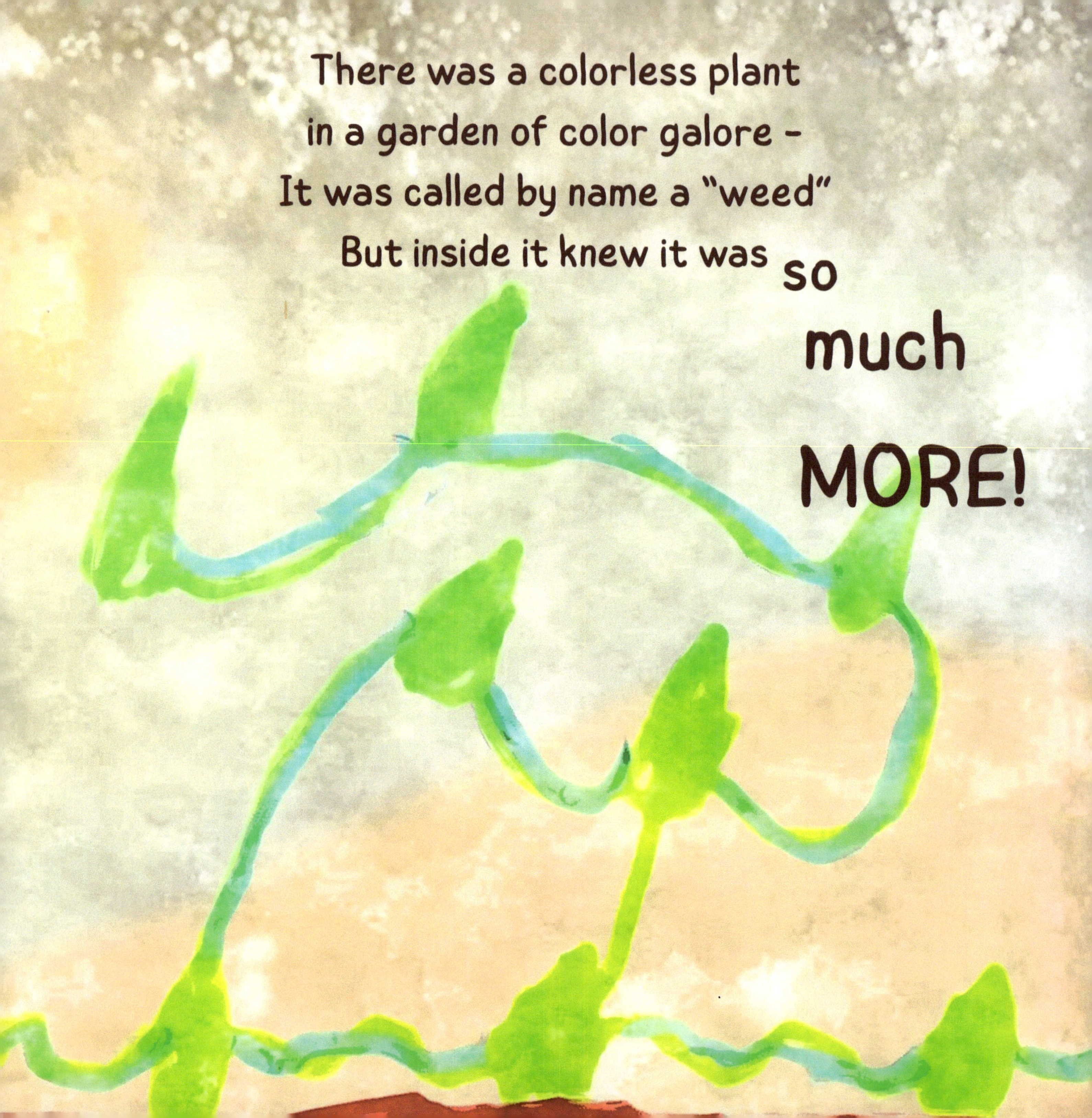

There was a colorless plant
in a garden of color galore -
It was called by name a "weed"
But inside it knew it was so much MORE!

All the other plants snuffed at its bare stems,
calling it simple & plain -
they wouldn't let PorterWeed dance,
sing or play with them in the rain!

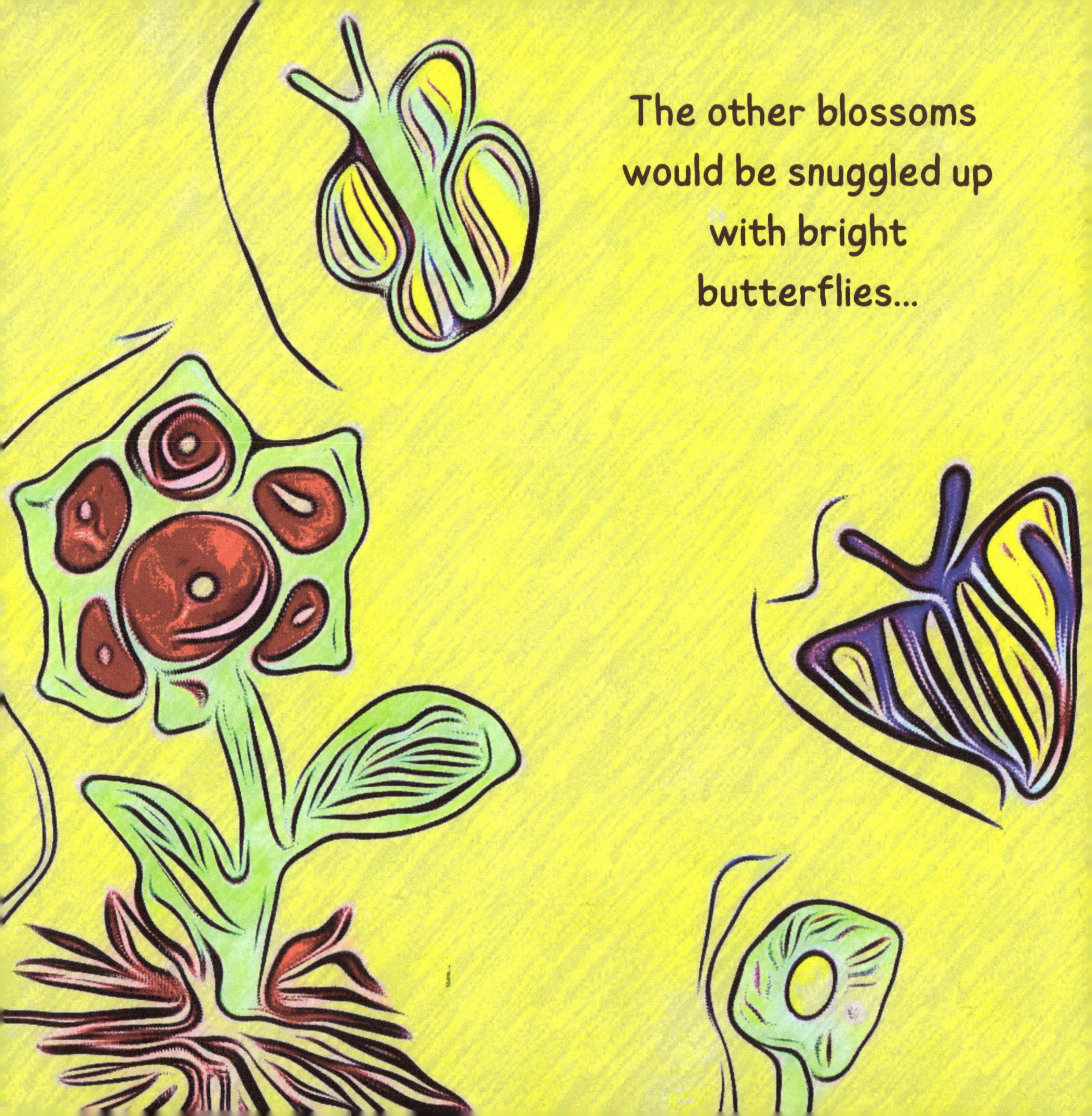

The other blossoms
would be snuggled up
with bright
butterflies...

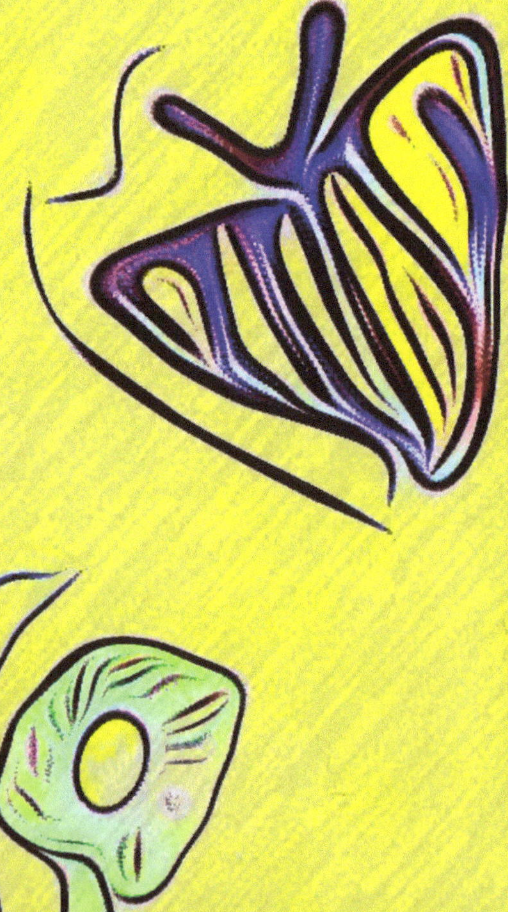

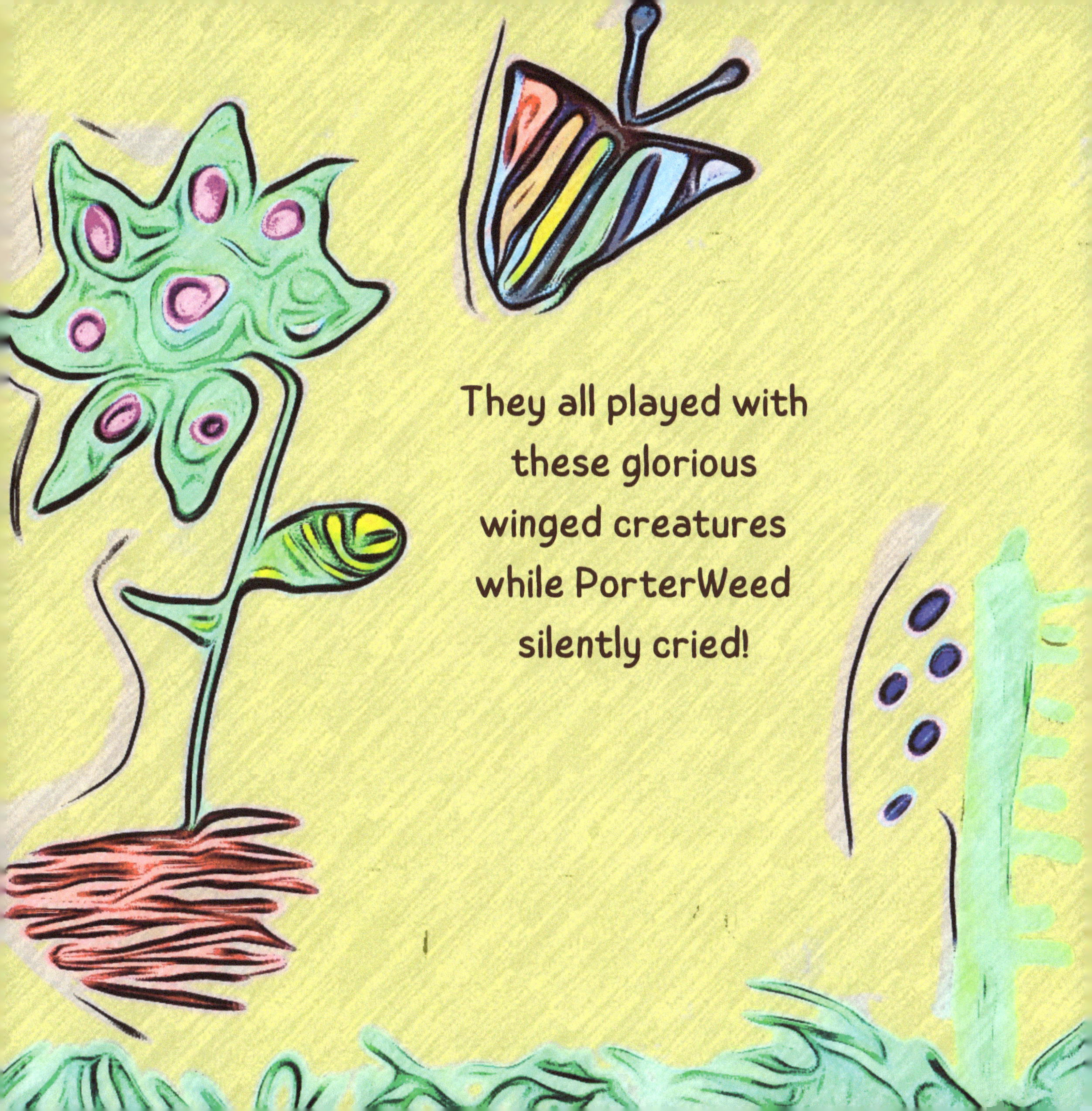

They all played with
these glorious
winged creatures
while PorterWeed
silently cried!

PorterWeed knew a truth
down in the depths of its Soul-
That it was born to be magical,
powerful & grow!

There was something calling
from deep within-
A voice growing louder
Wake up! Wake Up!
Little Plant!

It's time
to begin!

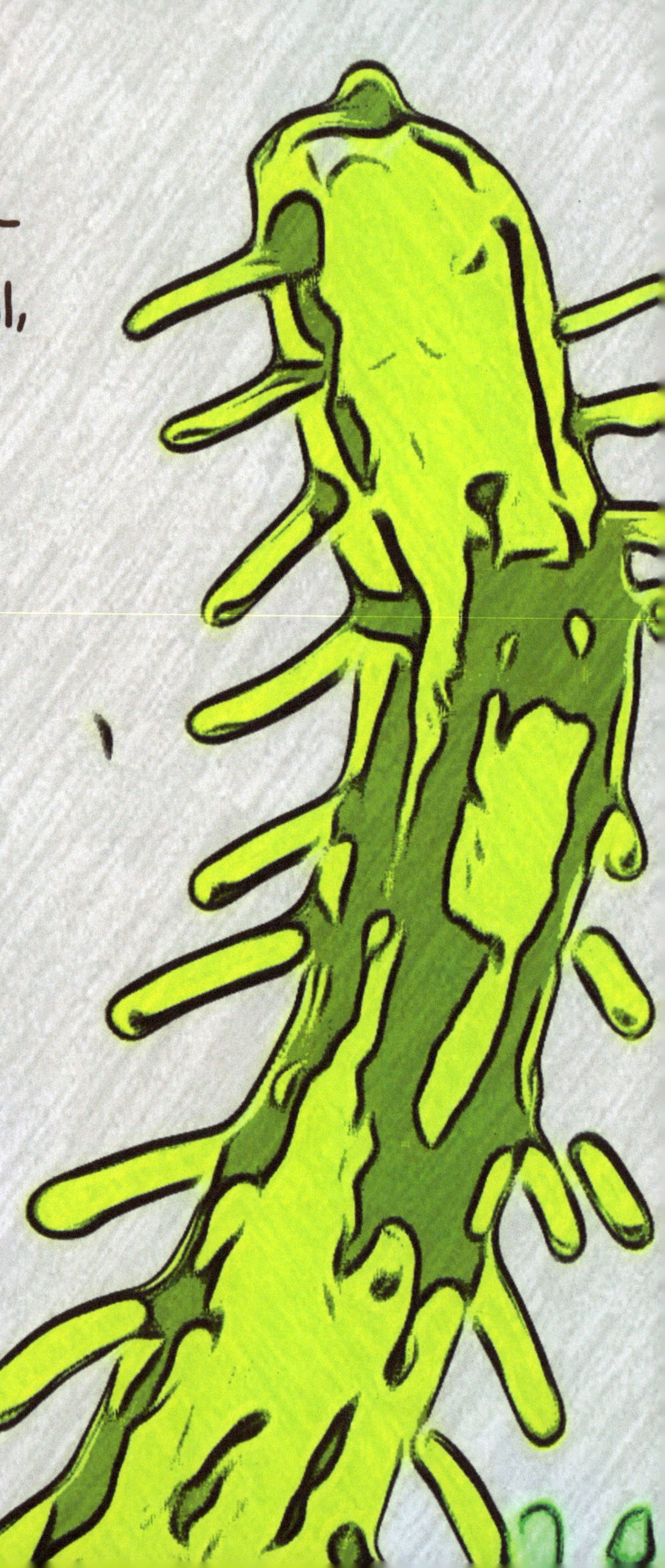

It's your Soul
beckoning you
To Rise-Up & Remember
Who You Really Are -

Its always been
inside of you.
Now its time to shine,
you budding superstar!

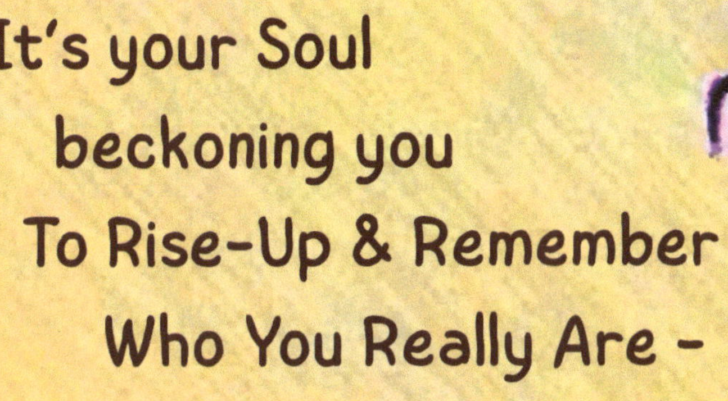

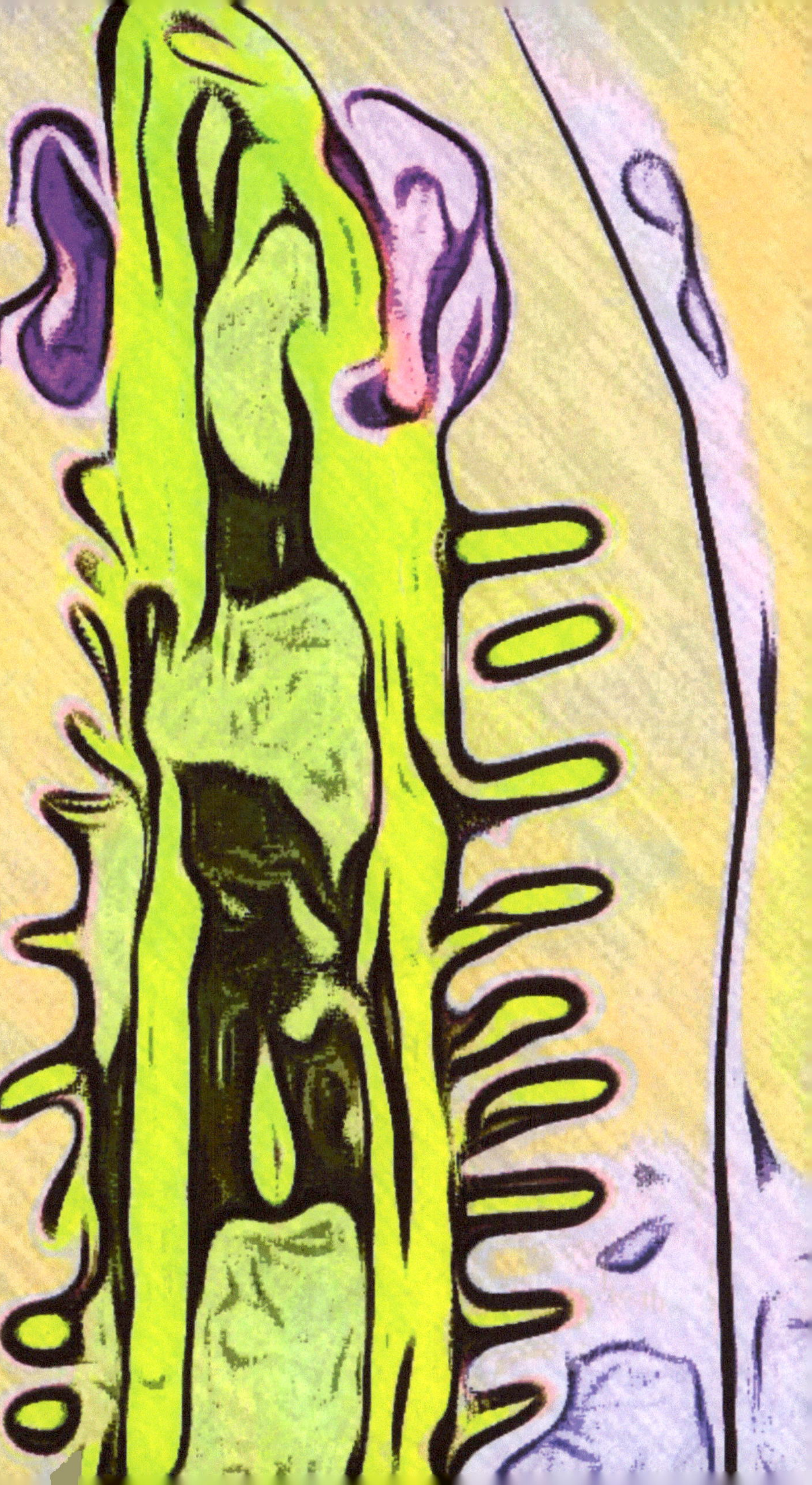

The mirror might reflect something
drab, dull or a bore -
But no more can you deny
the fierce force
brewing at your core!

Only YOU can Heed to
the calling inside-
IT MATTERS NOT
WHAT OTHERS THINK!
Let loose, dear one, your
brilliant,
sparkling
amethyst ink!

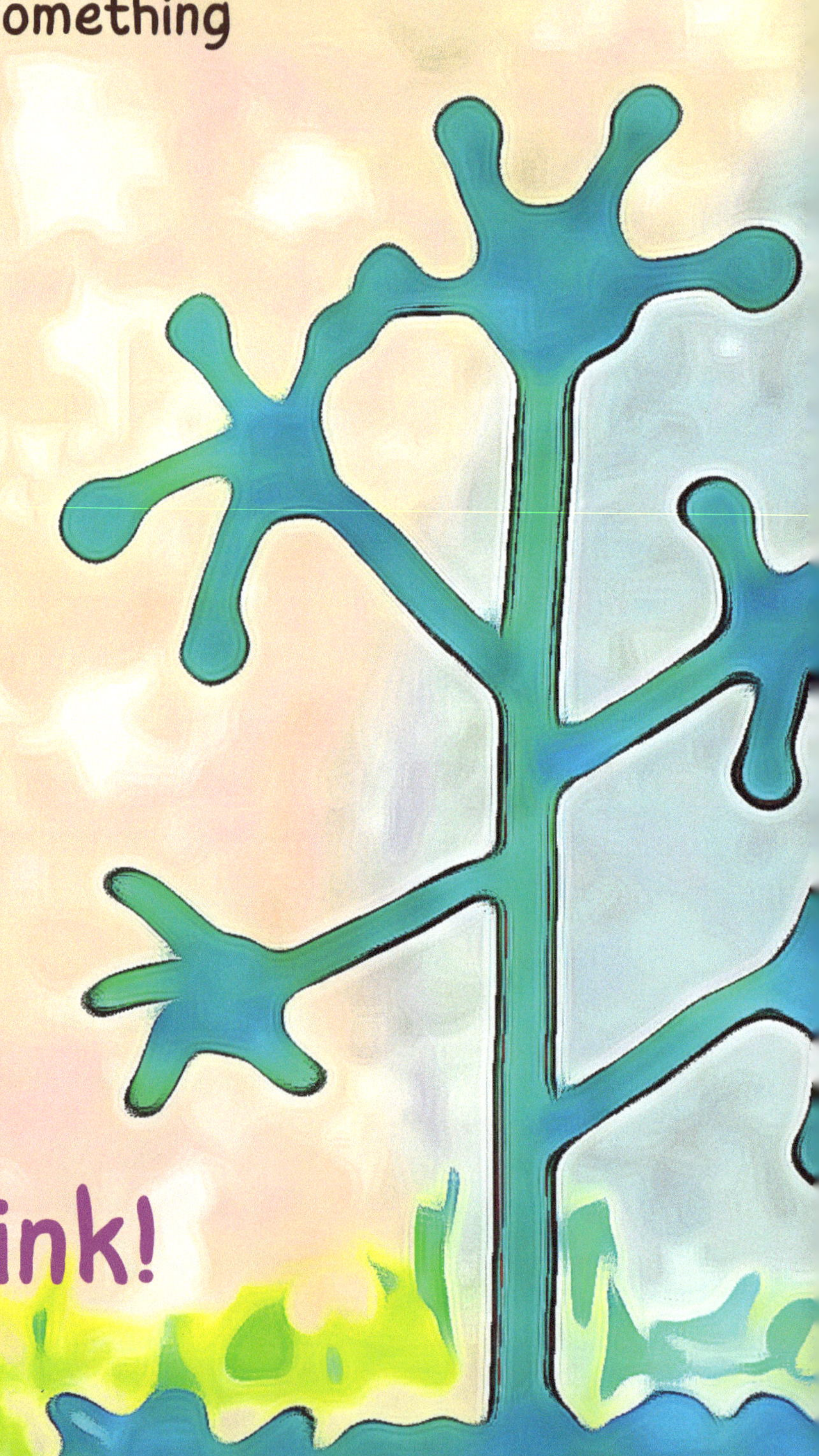

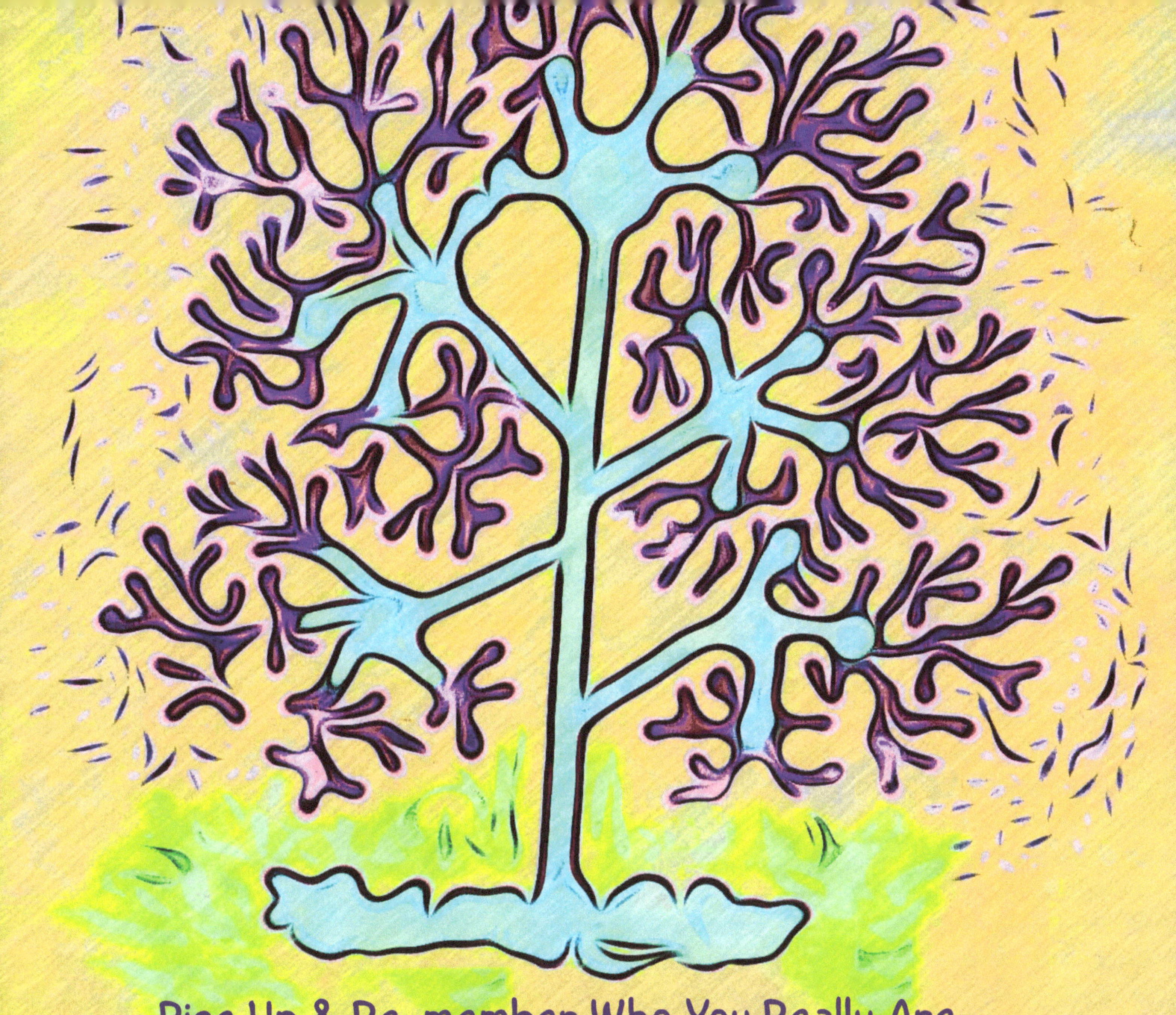

Rise Up & Re-member Who You Really Are-
Let your lackluster fade!
Into the heavenly pigment-
Into your true magnificent violet shade!

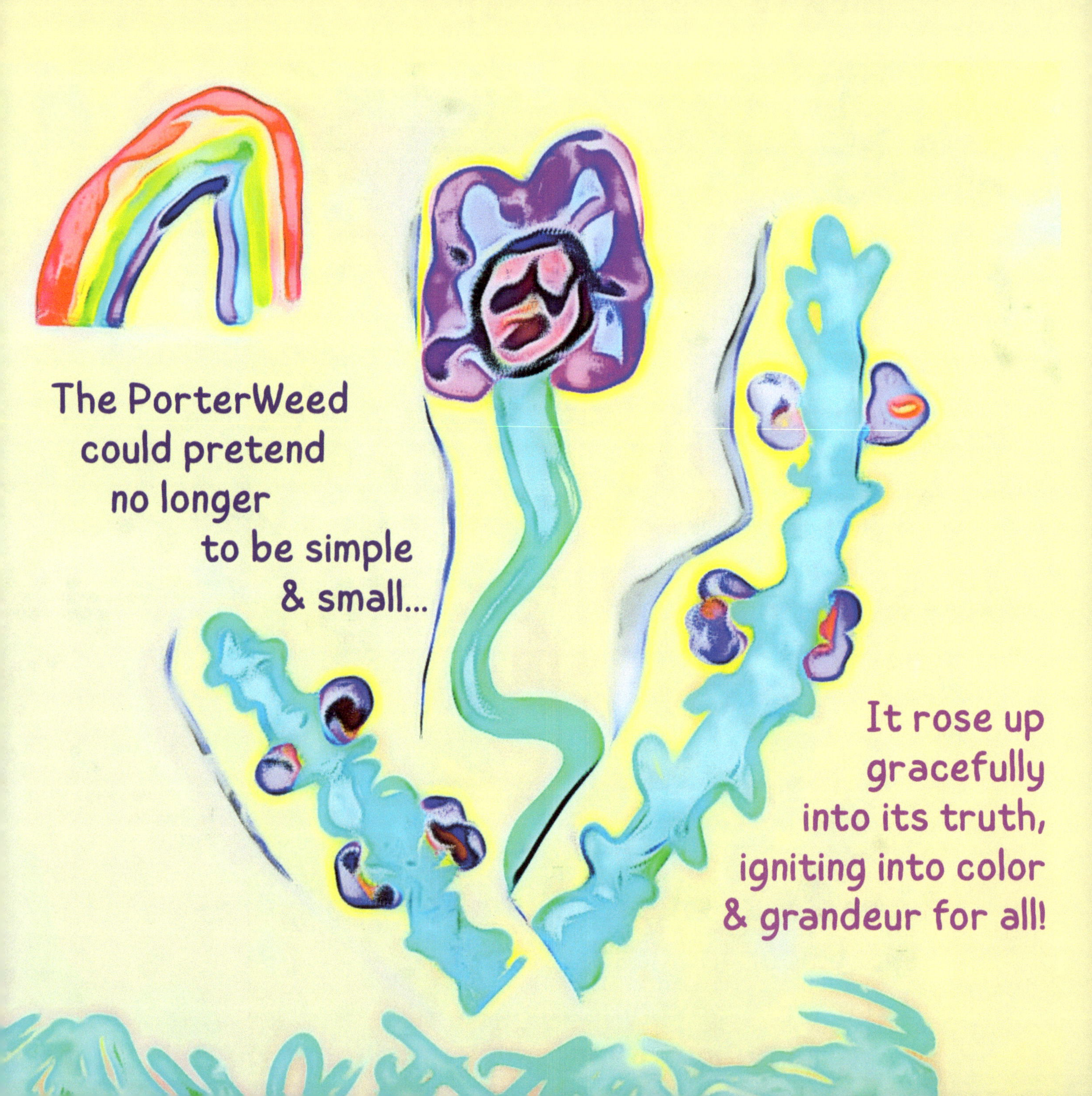
The PorterWeed
could pretend
no longer
to be simple
& small...

It rose up
gracefully
into its truth,
igniting into color
& grandeur for all!

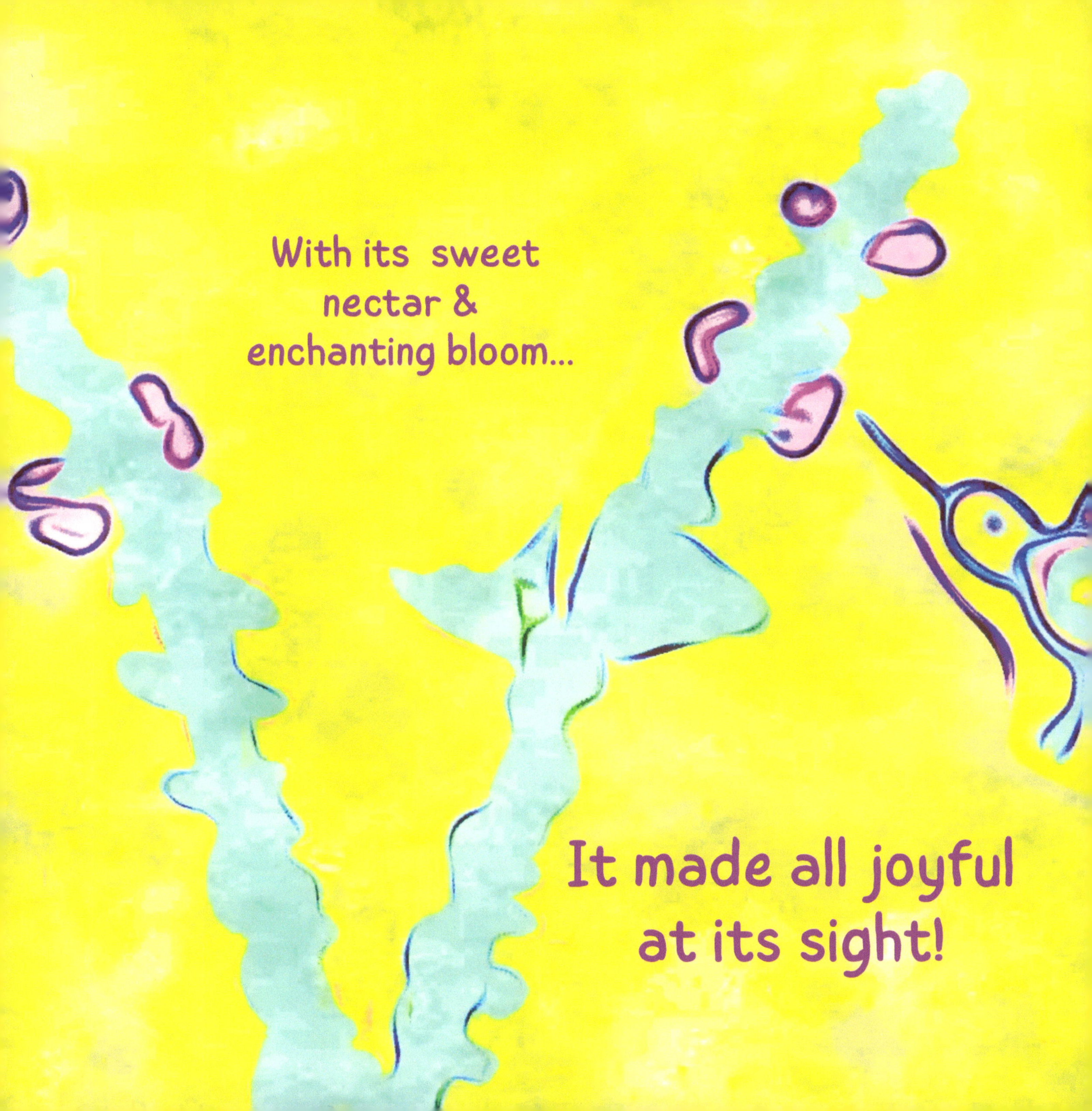
With its sweet
nectar &
enchanting bloom...

It made all joyful
at its sight!

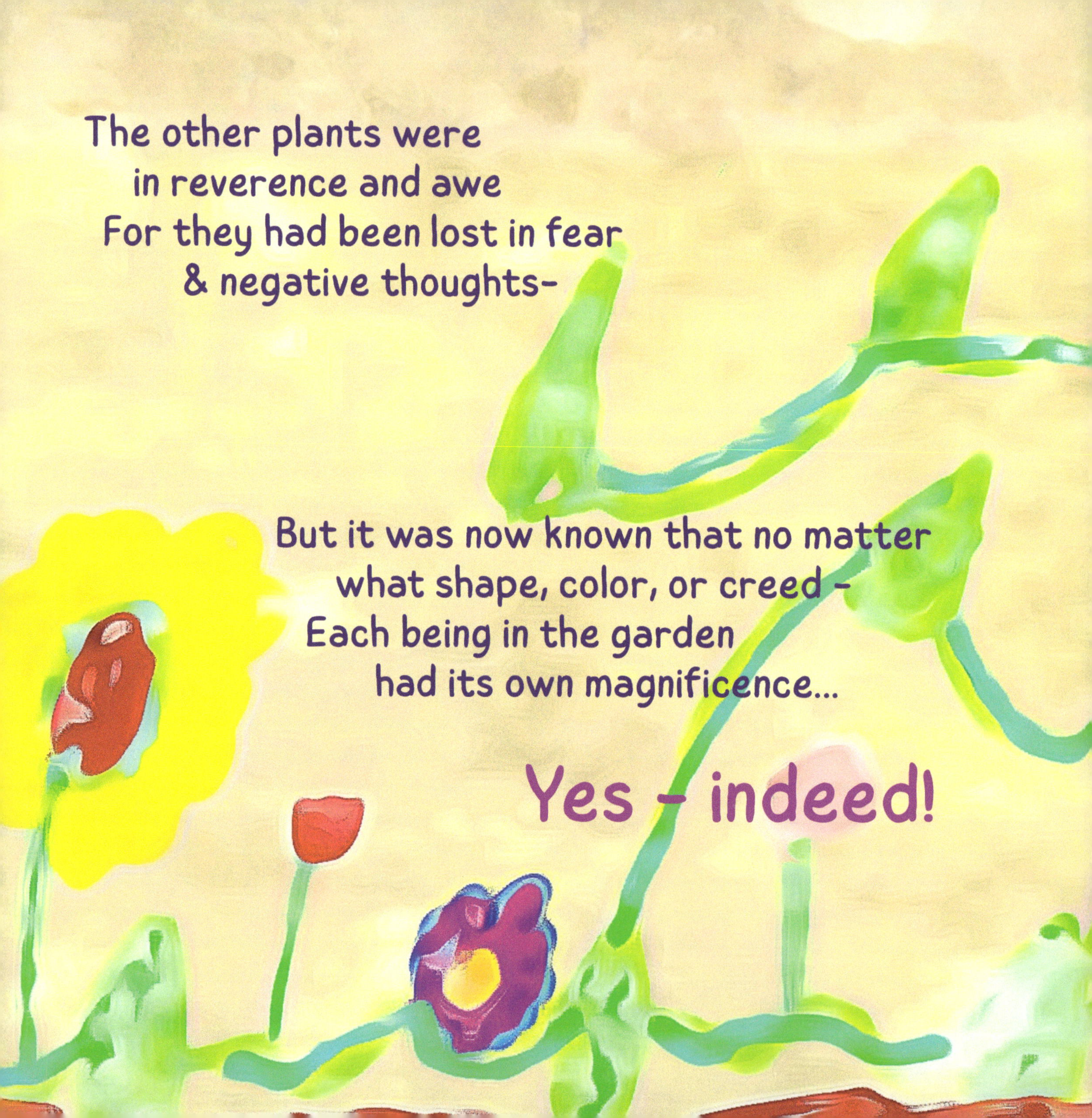
The other plants were
in reverence and awe
For they had been lost in fear
& negative thoughts-

But it was now known that no matter
what shape, color, or creed -
Each being in the garden
had its own magnificence...

Yes - indeed!

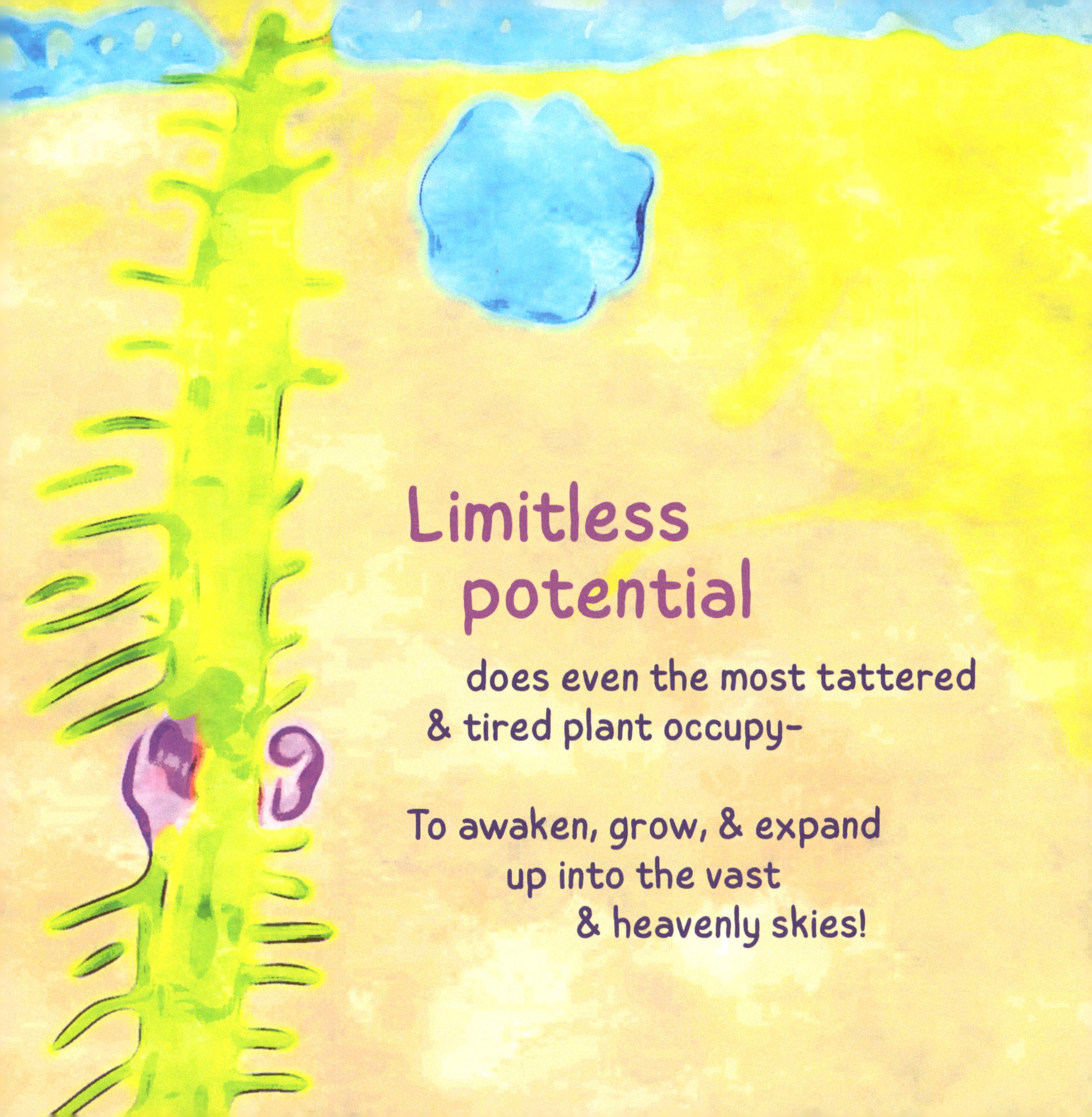

Limitless potential

does even the most tattered
& tired plant occupy-

To awaken, grow, & expand
up into the vast
& heavenly skies!

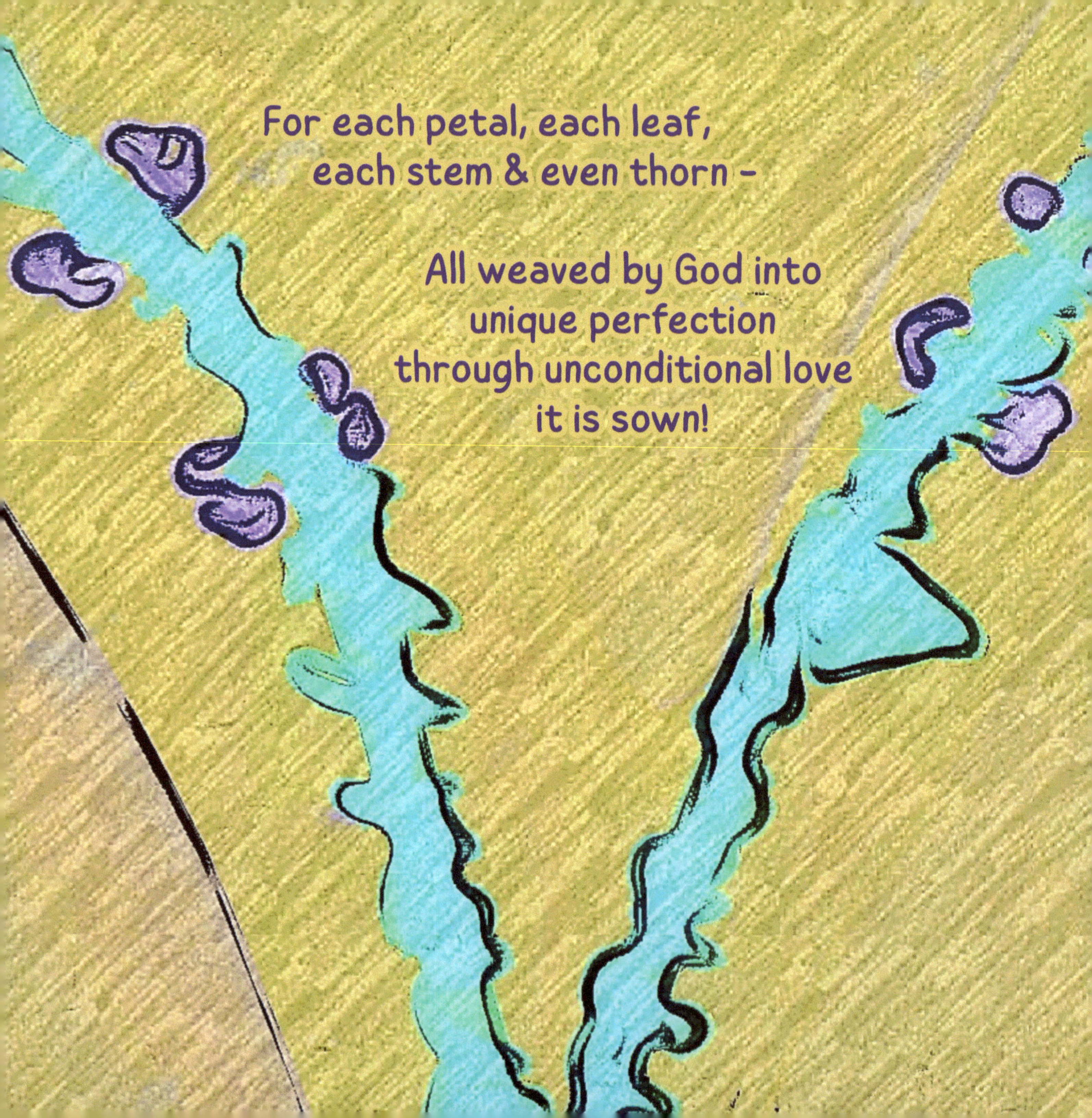
For each petal, each leaf,
each stem & even thorn -

All weaved by God into
unique perfection
through unconditional love
it is sown!

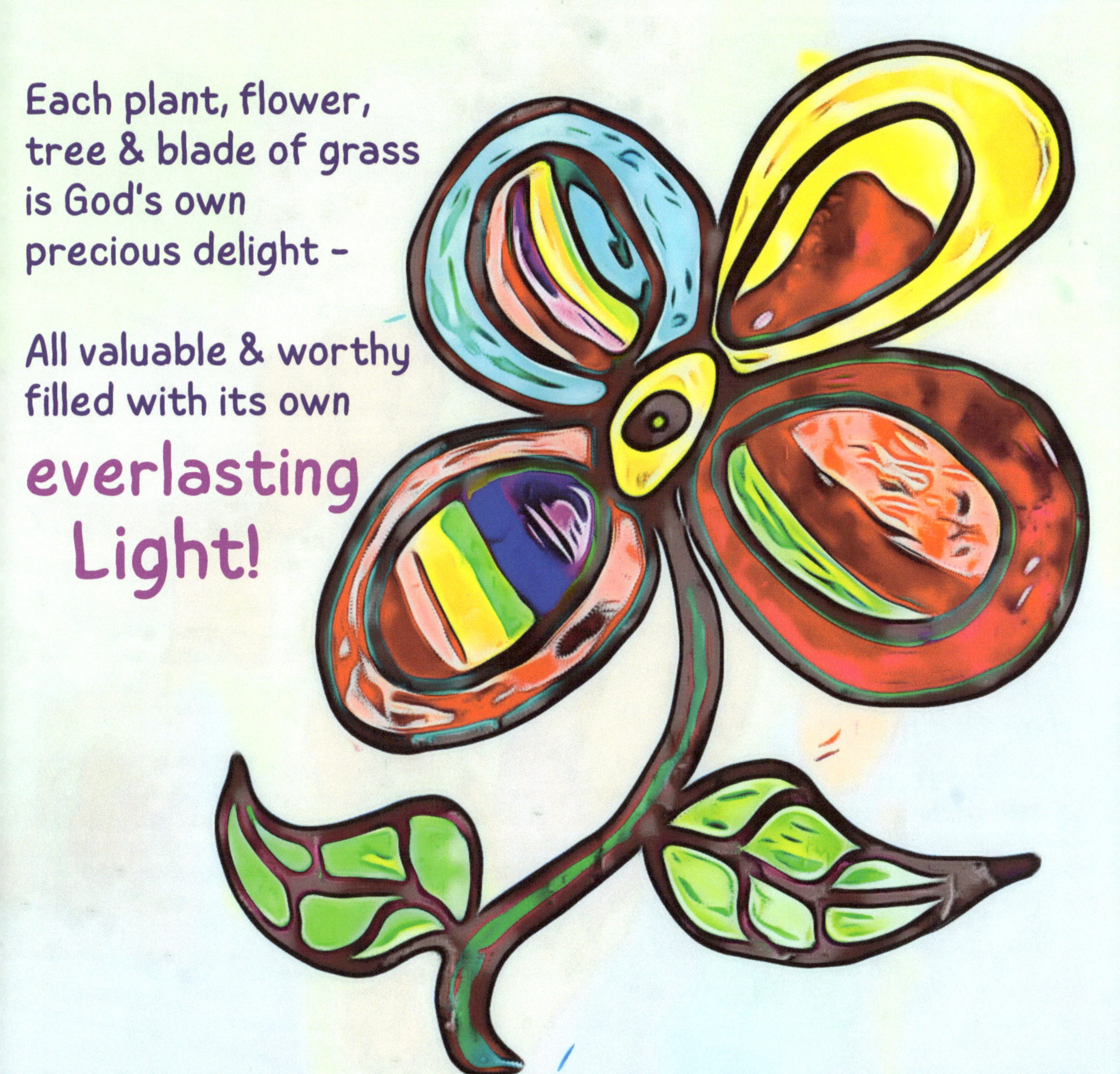

Each plant, flower,
tree & blade of grass
is God's own
precious delight –

All valuable & worthy
filled with its own
everlasting
Light!

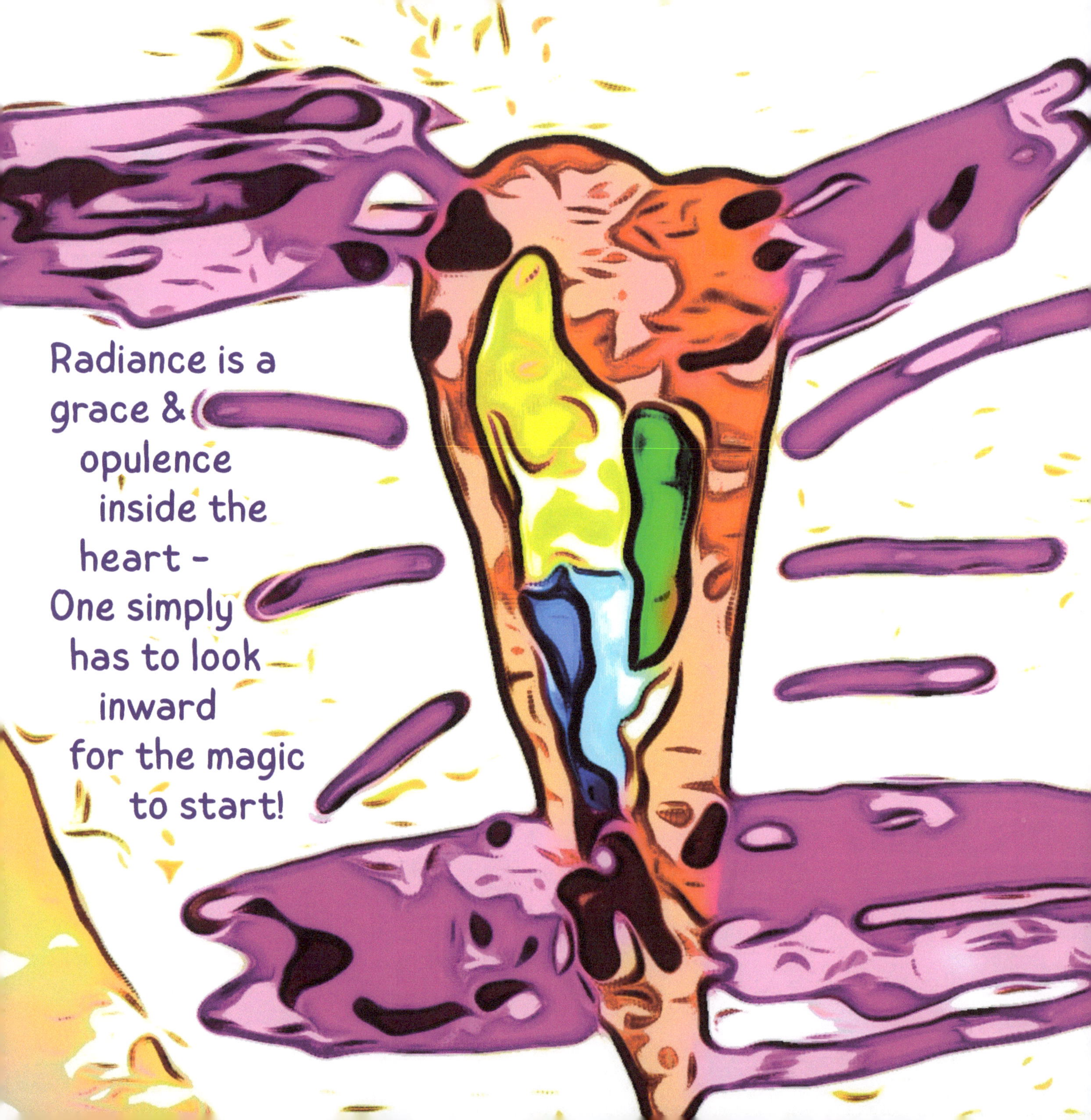

Radiance is a
grace &
opulence
inside the
heart -
One simply
has to look
inward
for the magic
to start!

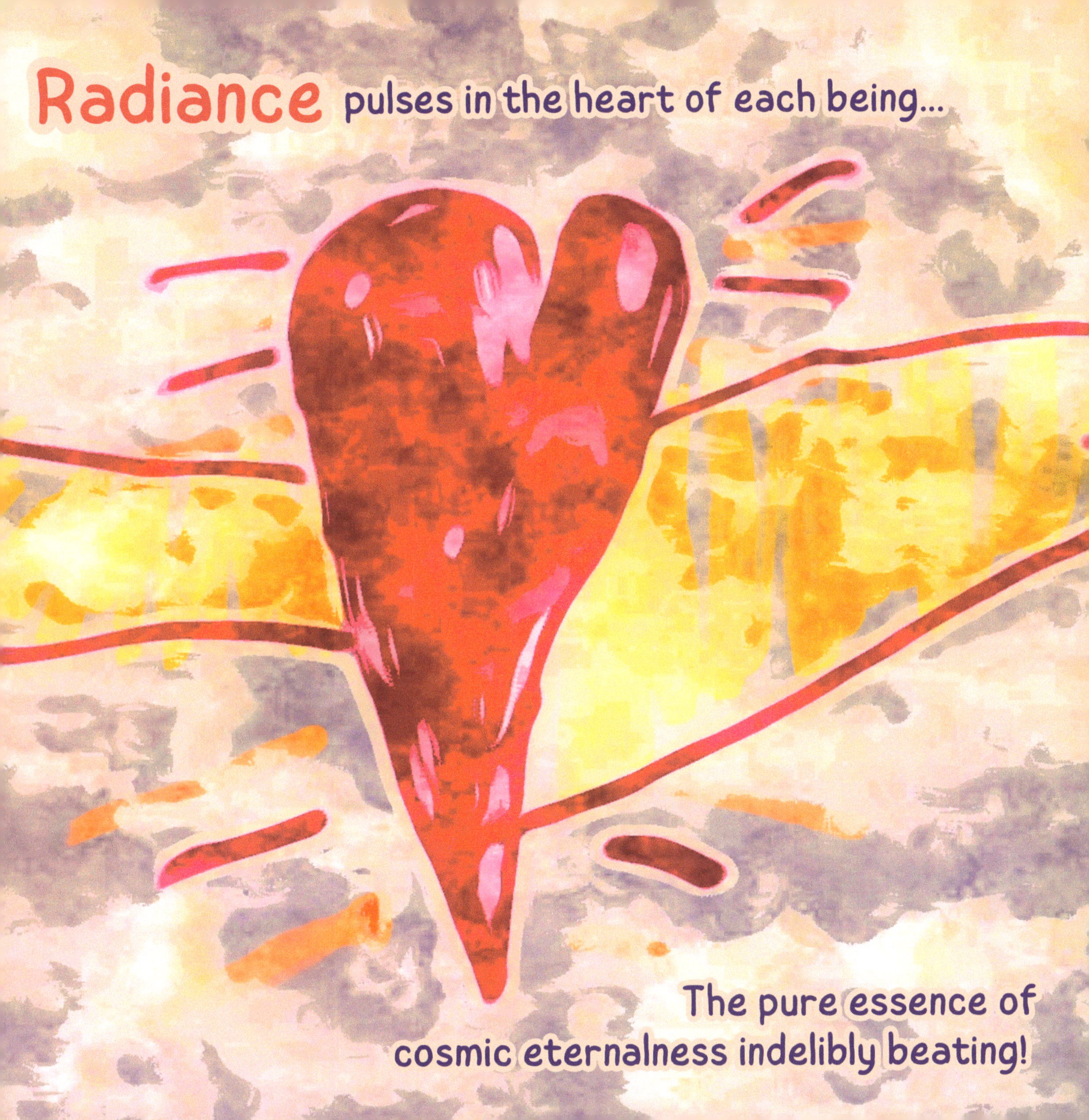
Radiance pulses in the heart of each being...
The pure essence of cosmic eternalness indelibly beating!

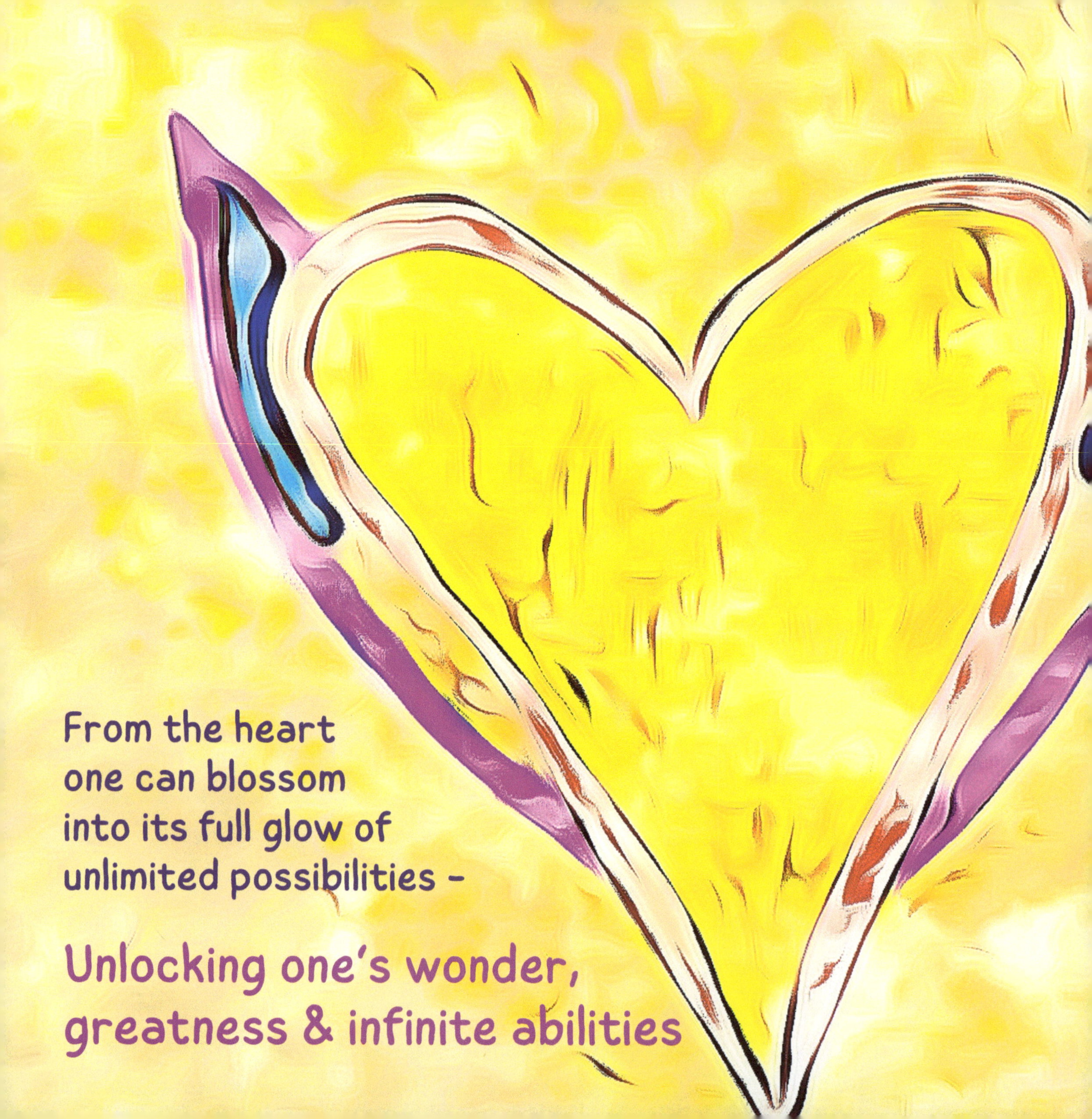
From the heart
one can blossom
into its full glow of
unlimited possibilities -

Unlocking one's wonder,
greatness & infinite abilities

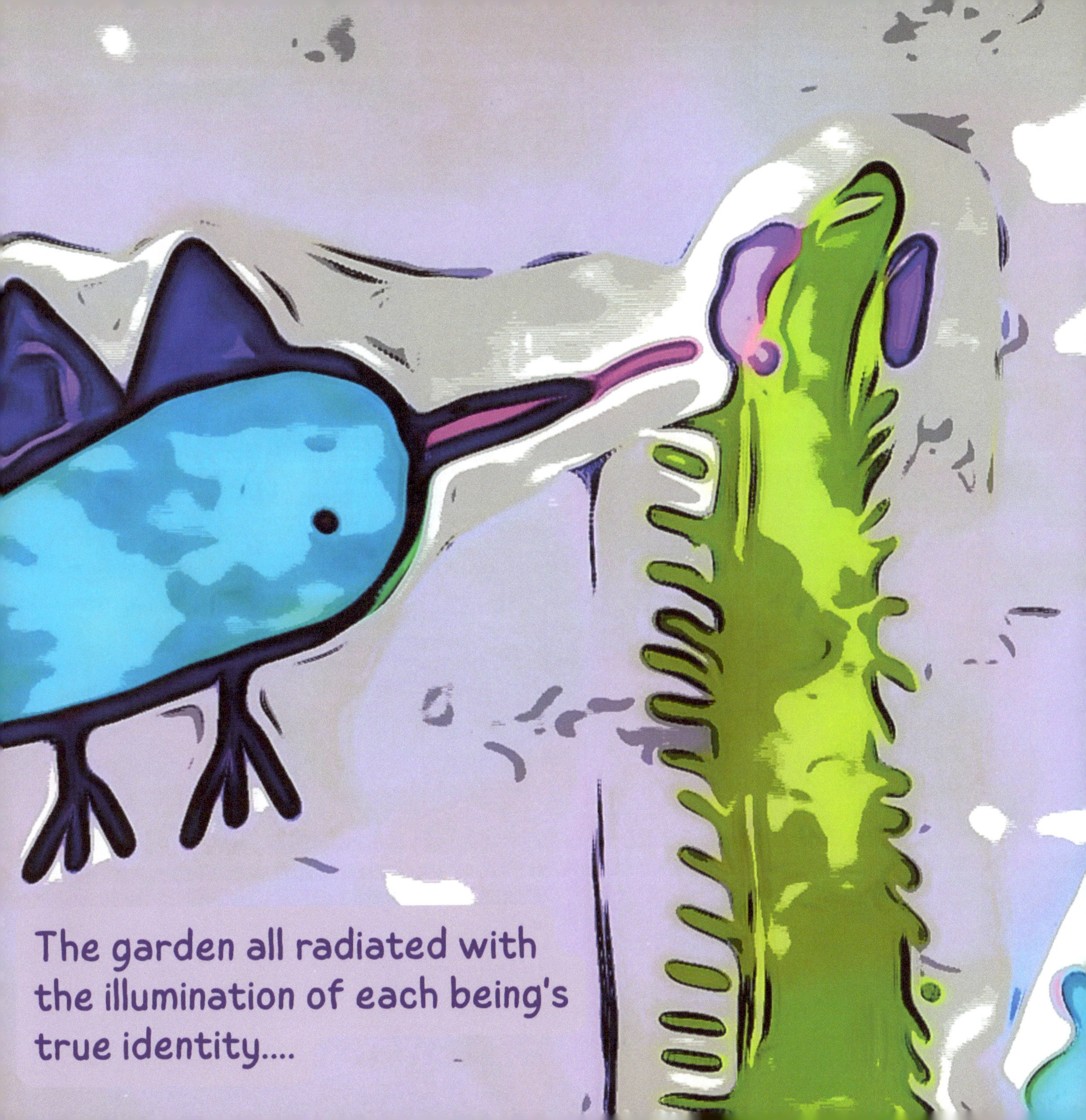

The garden all radiated with
the illumination of each being's
true identity....

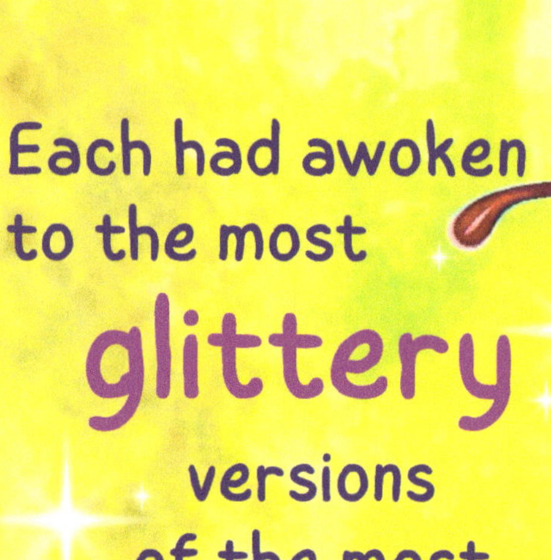

Each had awoken
to the most

glittery

versions
of the most

sparkly

visions
of who they
were born
to be.

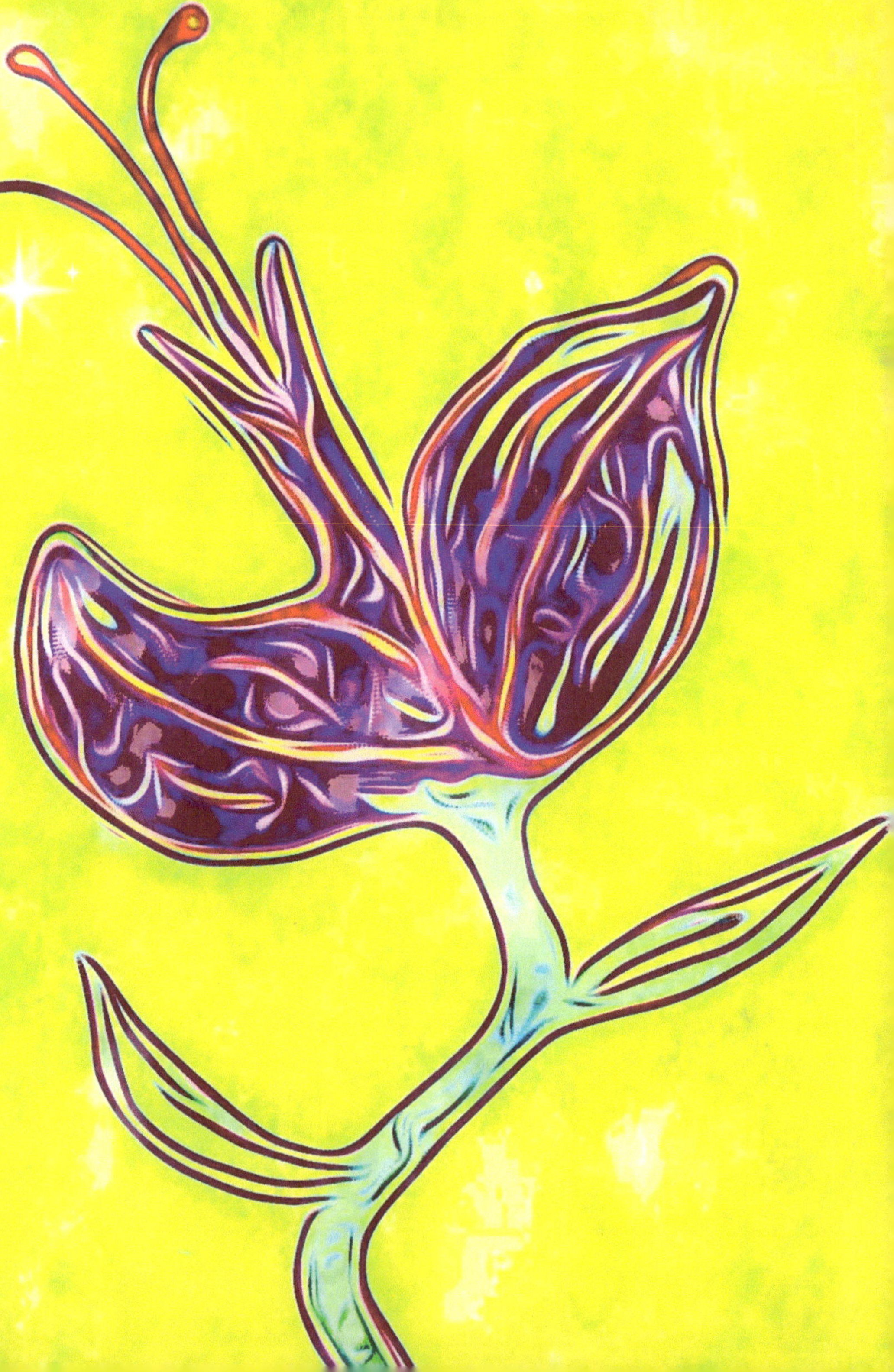

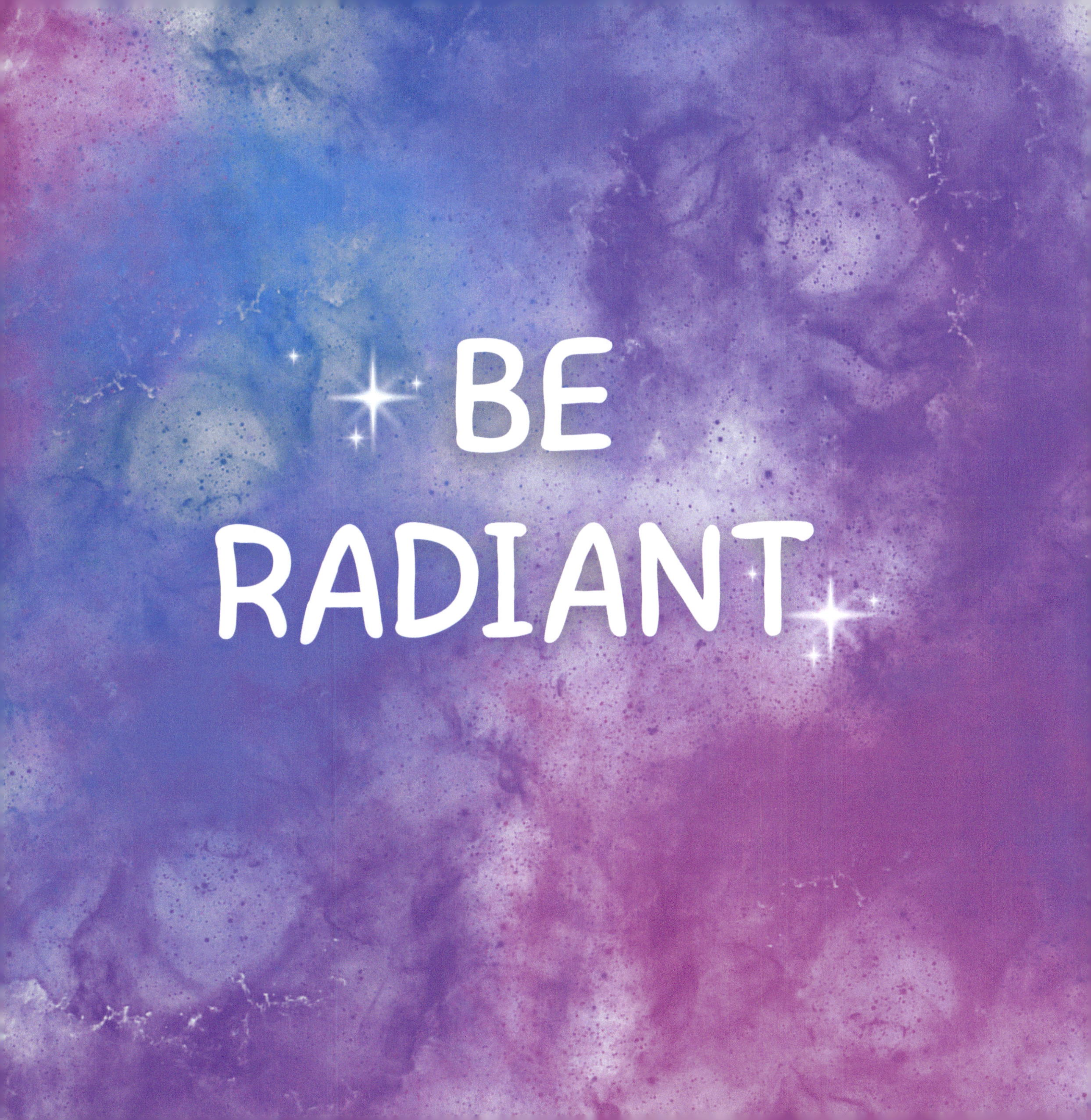

BE
RADIANT

www.ingramcontent.com/pod-product-compliance
Lightning Source LLC
Chambersburg PA
CBHW042145030726
47599CB00002B/621